THE DISASTROUS
WRANGEL ISLAND
EXPEDITION

by Katrina M. Phillips, Ph.D. • illustrated by Dave Shephard

CAPSTONE PRESS
a capstone imprint

Graphic Library is published by Capstone Press, an imprint of Capstone.
1710 Roe Crest Drive
North Mankato, Minnesota 56003
capstonepub.com

Library of Congress Cataloging-in-Publication Data
Names: Phillips, Katrina M., author. | Shephard, David (Illustrator), illustrator.
Title: The disastrous Wrangel Island expedition / by Katrina M. Phillips ; illustrated
by David Shephard.
Description: North Mankato, Minnesota : Capstone Press, an imprint of Capstone,
[2022] | Series: Deadly expeditions | Includes bibliographical references and
index. | Audience: Ages 8-11 | Audience: Grades 4-6 | Summary: "In 1921, Inupiat
seamstress Ada Blackjack joined a group of four white men who wanted to establish
a trading post on Wrangel Island in the freezing Arctic Ocean. The explorers were
stranded on the island when their return ship was forced to turn back due to ice.
Facing harsh conditions and dwindling food supplies, the men died one by one,
but Ada remained. Find out how she alone managed to survive the disastrous
expedition"— Provided by publisher.
Identifiers: LCCN 2021029786 (print) | LCCN 2021029787 (ebook) | ISBN
9781663958914 (hardcover) | ISBN 9781666322361 (paperback) | ISBN
9781666322378 (pdf) | ISBN 9781666322392 (kindle edition)
Subjects: LCSH: Blackjack, Ada, 1898-1983—Juvenile literature. | Inuit women—
Biography—Juvenile literature. | Inuit—Biography—Juvenile literature. | Wrangel
Island (Russia)—Discovery and exploration—Juvenile literature. | Arctic regions—
Discovery and exploration—Juvenile literature. | Wilderness survival—Russia
(Federation)—Wrangel Island—Juvenile literature. | Women explorers—Arctic
regions—Biography—Juvenile literature. | Explorers—Arctic regions—Biography—
Juvenile literature.
Classification: LCC E99.E7 P474 2022 (print) | LCC E99.E7 (ebook) | DDC 910.92
[B]—dc23
LC record available at https://lccn.loc.gov/2021029786
LC ebook record available at https://lccn.loc.gov/2021029787

Editorial Credits
Editor: Mandy Robbins; Designer: Dina Her; Media Researcher: Jo Miller;
Production Specialist: Tori Abraham

All internet sites appearing in back matter were available and accurate when this
book was sent to press.

TABLE OF CONTENTS

Ada Deletuk was born in 1898 in a small village near Nome, Alaska. Her family was Inuit. They are Alaska's Native people.

At a young age, Ada learned the traditional stories passed down by her people. Some stories told of gods and goddesses who lived in the sea. Others taught about the stars in the night sky. One story told of Nanook, the king of the polar bears. Inuit legends taught children to fear polar bears. Ada would carry these stories with her for the rest of her life.

When Ada was eight years old, tragedy struck. Her father died.

Ada's mother sent her and her sister Rita to be raised by white Methodist missionaries. Instead of learning Inuit skills for surviving in the Arctic wilderness, Ada learned basic reading and writing in English. She also learned to cook and sew.

At the age of 16, Ada married Jack Blackjack. He was a dogsled driver. The couple had three children, but two died.

In 1921, Jack abandoned Ada and their 5-year-old son, Bennett, in the Alaskan wilderness.

COUGH!

It's OK, son. I've got you.

Ada Blackjack walked about 40 miles (64 kilometers) back to Nome. Bennett suffered from tuberculosis. The disease made it difficult for the boy to breathe. She carried him much of the way.

Back in Nome, Blackjack faced a difficult decision. She had to make money to pay for treatments for her son's illness, but she couldn't work and care for him at the same time. She was forced to place him in an orphanage.

GENERAL STORE

GENERAL STORE

THE JESSE LEE HOME FOR CHILDREN

Mama!

We will take good care of him.

I will be back for you, my boy. I will make money and come get you!

Blackjack took on work as a seamstress. She mended people's clothing and did other odd jobs, but it didn't pay enough to help her son.

I need to make more money! But how?

Meanwhile, aging explorer Vilhjalmur Stefansson was wrestling with his own frustrations.

I need men to go on an expedition for me! I will show the world that the Arctic is a friendly place to live!

Stefansson was born in Manitoba, Canada, in 1879. His parents had come from Iceland. His family moved to North Dakota, in the United States, where Stefansson grew up. But he could never shake his fascination with his northern heritage. In 1906, he signed on to be part of an Arctic expedition. When the rest of his group failed to meet him, Stefansson spent the winter with the Inuit people. There he learned about their way of life.

Stefansson became obsessed with the idea of Europeans living in the Arctic. He wanted to establish a colony to be a center for trade in the Arctic. He was certain that if the Europeans lived in the same manner as the Inuit, they could make it happen.

If only my fellow explorers would listen to me and live like the Native people do, we could start a colony in the Arctic.

Between 1906 and 1918, Stefansson went on three expeditions to the Arctic. They included the disastrous Canadian Arctic Expedition, in which the ship the *Karluk* was lost. Its passengers were stranded on a place called Wrangel Island for six months.

Stefansson was interested in Wrangel Island. It was 600 miles (966 km) north of Nome, surrounded by the Chukchi Sea.

The island was home to many animals. If polar bears, sea creatures, birds, and foxes could call this land home, why not humans? Stefansson was determined to find people willing to start a settlement there.

To teach people about surviving in the Arctic, Stefansson joined the Chautauqua circuit. This group of people traveled the United States, informing and entertaining crowds. There, Stefansson worked with Fred Maurer. Maurer had been part of an earlier Stefansson expedition. His ship got stuck near Wrangel Island in 1914. Stefansson went for help. By the time he returned, the ship had drifted away. The survivors, including Maurer, were stranded on Wrangel Island for six long months before they were rescued.

I need men for another mission to Wrangel. You know what it's like up there, Fred. Would you go?

I buried three friends on Wrangel, sir. I want to go back to prove their deaths were not in vain.

Will you be coming too?

No. I will stay back and raise money for more supplies and further exploration.

Mr. Stefansson? Sir? I hear you're planning to send explorers to the Arctic. Please, consider me.

You've done an excellent job running the projector for the show, Milton, but this is much more challenging. Do you really think you're up for it?

When the Chautauqua show stopped in New Braunfels, Texas, young Milton Galle joined Stefansson's team. He was 19 years old and dreaming of adventure.

Stefansson also asked Lorne Knight to join the crew. Knight had explored the Arctic with Stefansson in 1917 and was eager to go back.

I think I know the answer to my question, but would you go to the Arctic again?

I keep telling you, I need to go back.

Stefansson wrote to people all over the country looking for able-bodied explorers. Dr. W.A. Park at the University of Toronto suggested the expedition to his student Allan Crawford. Crawford jumped at the chance.

Dear Sir: I was given your letter about the three-year polar expedition. I have studied geology, and I have the expertise you need for this journey.

Stefansson's goal was to send his crew to Wrangel Island for a two-year expedition. But he only sent them with six months' worth of supplies.

The crew's ability to survive on their own would prove his theory that Europeans could live in the Arctic. There were plans, however, for a ship to resupply them after one year.

This feels good. I'll take this one.

Yes, sir. I'll get your ammunition.

The crew stopped in Seattle, Washington, to buy most of their supplies. They needed hunting equipment and warm clothes.

We still need socks, pants, boots, mitts, and handkerchiefs.

The crew boarded the *Victoria* and set sail for Nome. Stefansson had told the men to keep their destination a secret to stop other parties from claiming Wrangel Island first.

Well that's most of it. What else is on our list?

One of those animal skin rowboats–for hunting. What are they called?

An umiak.

We'll recruit them at our next stop: Nome, Alaska.

And we need to hire Inuit families–men to hunt and women to sew warm winter clothing of animal skins.

Where are you headed, boys?

The North Pole.

I don't know. They haven't told me yet.

Ellesmere Island.

Aren't you working for that Stefansson fellow? I wouldn't trust him as far as I could throw him.

When the men arrived in Nome, the crew of the *Victoria* gave them a kitten for good luck. Many sailors believed cats were good luck.

Here you go fellas! Good luck, wherever you're going.

Let's call her "Vic," after the ship.

They're gonna need all the luck they can get.

Stefansson had told them to buy an umiak in Nome. This skin boat was for hunting. It was light enough to carry, but could hold 2 to 3 tons. The men could bring back a seal or a walrus in this boat.

How much? That's robbery!

That's the price. You can take it or leave it.

I know a place in Siberia where we won't have to pay this much.

Stefansson had also stressed the importance of having Inuit men and women join the expedition to hunt, cook, and sew. These Native people knew how to survive the brutal Arctic conditions.

We need some families to join us.

To help us hunt, cook, and sew warm clothing. We will pay you well!

I don't trust them. They won't even say where they're going.

These fellows aren't prepared for a year in the Arctic.

Police Chief E.R. Jordan knew Blackjack and the trouble she faced.

There is a group of men exploring the Arctic for at least a year. They need a seamstress to sew clothes.

They are hiring entire families—men to hunt and women to cook and sew.

I don't want to be the only Inuit with these white men—or the only woman!

A year is so long to be away! And think of all the polar bears in the wilderness!

14

We don't really need an umiak, boys.

I know how to hunt polar bears, seals, and foxes without a big boat.

Let's get the small skin boat instead. And we can get the wooden dory from the *Silver Wave*.

Then the men tried to find more Native people to join the expedition.

No luck. No one we spoke to would come with us.

We couldn't find anyone either. I guess it's just you, Ada.

What have I gotten myself into?

17

The *Silver Wave* left Blackjack and the four men on Wrangel Island early on the morning of September 16, 1921. Unfortunately, the small skin boat the men had bought in Siberia had been lost in a storm during the trip.

At first, the island seemed welcoming. The temperatures were above freezing, and there were mosses and other small plants, though no trees. Animal tracks promised plenty of wildlife. The men set to work digging out the side of a hill. Inside the dugout, they pitched three tents—one for supplies, one as a kitchen and for Blackjack to sleep in, and one for the men to sleep in.

In the following weeks the group settled into a routine. The men taught themselves to shoot and set up fox traps. They hunted wild animals and brought them back to camp.

Blackjack cooked up whatever meat the men brought back. Polar bear steak became a favorite dish, even though it reminded Blackjack of her great fear.

Why must there be so many polar bears on this island?

She sewed warm winter clothing from the animal skins. The crew would need them to go out in the deadly winter temperatures.

The men also mapped the island, as Stefansson had instructed them to.

They studied the island's wildlife and weather patterns. They took notes to take back.

Though there were no trees on the island, there was plenty of driftwood that had washed in from the sea. The men spent time collecting it for fires and building supplies.

As winter grew near, the men built a frame out of driftwood planks.

When the snow came, the men built walls for their winter house out of snow blocks. They moved the tents inside this shelter and built a storm shed in front of it to hold supplies.

As winter set in and the days grew shorter, most of the animals left Wrangel Island. The group soon ran out of meat.

Any luck?

We shot a walrus, but we couldn't get it back in the dory.

If only we had an umiak!

The group settled in for a long, cold winter. Temperatures dipped below 0 degrees Fahrenheit (minus 18 degrees Celsius) and stayed there. The sun set and didn't rise again for two months. The group had enough food to last until spring. They weren't worried. They knew a supply ship would come to restock them in the summer.

It's OK. We should have enough food to last us through the winter. Then the animals will come back.

And the supply boat will come next summer.

By April, the group had grown eager for the supply ship to reach them, but the ice around the island had yet to melt.

I wonder when the supply ship will arrive.

Not until this blasted ice melts!

In the meantime, we're low on wood. Let's move the camp to where we can find more.

In May, the group moved their camp to a new location. Food supplies grew low. There were still few animals to hunt, except for seals. But they couldn't bring such a large animal back to shore without an umiak.

I hope the men have luck hunting soon. All we have left is some rice and bread.

But as summer drew to an end, no ship came. The group became worried.

Look at all that ice! How will the supply ship get through?

I have a bad feeling too.

Maybe they can sled across the ice to us.

I don't think so. I've got a bad feeling they're not coming.

We need to move our camp again and start stocking up on wood and meat for the winter.

Little did the explorers trapped on Wrangel Island know, but their supply ship, the *Teddy Bear*, had been forced to turn back.

Captain, what are we going to do? There's too much ice.

We have to turn around. We'll never reach the island.

The group built another winter camp, surrounding the tents with ice blocks to keep out the bitter cold. They tried to hunt game, but once again, the animals were scarce. They did manage to get a walrus, which fed them for some time.

This is the last of the walrus meat. We'll have nothing but the skin to chew on when it's gone.

I will try to make it last.

Come on in and rest, Lorne. You don't look so good.

Lorne Knight was not doing well. He had developed a disease called scurvy. He'd had it before. It is caused by lack of vitamin C. Symptoms are weakness, swollen limbs, and bleeding gums. If not treated, it's deadly.

By Christmas, Knight and Crawford decided to go for help.

I think I have scurvy again, Allan. I don't know if I'll last another winter here.

It's time we go for help. We can take the dogsled over the ice to Nome.

Crawford and Knight set out for Nome on January 7, 1923, with five dogs and a dogsled loaded with supplies. The journey would take at least two months in subzero temperatures in the dark.

Lorne, we have to go back!

No! We must keep going.

You're too sick. You'll never make it.

On January 20, the two men returned to the camp on Wrangel Island. Knight was too sick to make the trip.

On January 28, Crawford, Galle, and Maurer decided to try for help again. Knight stayed behind. He had convinced the others to go and that he was well enough to help Blackjack tend camp.

You and Lorne will be fine, Ada.

We'll be back. I promise.

Goodbye, Ada.

Be careful, and hurry back!

But Knight wasn't fine. His symptoms were getting worse.

What happened? Are you OK?

No, I don't think I am.

With Knight sick and the other men gone, Blackjack had to do it all. She taught herself to trap foxes. The meat would help Knight's condition.

Did you eat your soup?

I can't. It hurts too much to move.

Blackjack did everything she could to help Knight and keep the camp going over the long, lonely months. Knight was in pain and afraid. He didn't always appreciate her work, and he was sometimes cruel.

Let me help you.

I don't want your help!

By May, Blackjack had convinced herself that she needed to learn to shoot a gun. Then she could hunt and defend herself against the dreaded polar bears.

I can do this. Just pull the trigger!

Blackjack's fear almost became a reality one day while hunting seals. A polar bear surprised her from behind! Luckily, the hungry bear only chose to swipe the seal she had just shot.

Blackjack didn't want to be snuck up on again. She built a platform from which she could shoot any polar bears that came near camp.

Despite her best efforts, Knight's condition grew worse. In his weakened state, Knight spoke gently to Blackjack.

Be strong, Ada. I won't make it, but I know you will.

On June 22, 1923, he died.

Blackjack was too small to move Knight. She covered his body and blocked the entrance to the tent to keep out the animals on the island. Then she moved everything she needed to survive into the storage tent.

With her only human companion gone, Blackjack knew she had to survive on her own. It was her only chance at ever seeing Bennett again. The Inuit woman who had never learned the traditional survival skills of her people proved she could survive the harsh conditions. Her hunting skills continued to improve.

She even managed to kill a seal from a skin boat that she made herself.

With the sealskin, she kept busy sewing. She focused her mind on the thought of seeing her son again.

I wonder if these shoes will even fit Bennett when I see him again.

Finally, on August 20th, Blackjack spotted a ship in the distance.

Is it possible? Could I really be saved?

The ship was called the *Donaldson*. Captain Harold Noice brought supplies, along with 13 more people to colonize Wrangel Island. Assuming the original party was doing fine, Stefansson wanted to grow the colony. No one was prepared for the disastrous outcome of the expedition.

Are the men with you? Where are Allan, Fred, and Milton?

Aren't they here?

Blackjack then realized that Crawford, Galle, and Maurer had not survived their trek to get help. She was heartbroken that the men were dead.

They went for help in January. Lorne died in June. It's just been me ever since.

The sailors of the *Donaldson* surveyed the area before taking Blackjack back to Nome. They were impressed with her survival skills.

I can't believe that little woman kept up the camp on her own for two months.

I bet she could have lasted another winter.

Blackjack's sadness turned to joy when she finally reunited with her son in Nome.

Mama!

Bennett!

Blackjack never received the full payment she was promised, but she did get enough to treat Bennett's illness. Blackjack married again and had another son, Billy, in 1924. She spent most of the rest of her life in Alaska. Ada Blackjack Johnson died on May 29, 1983. The state of Alaska officially honored her as a local hero on June 16, 1983.

MAP OF THE EXPEDITION

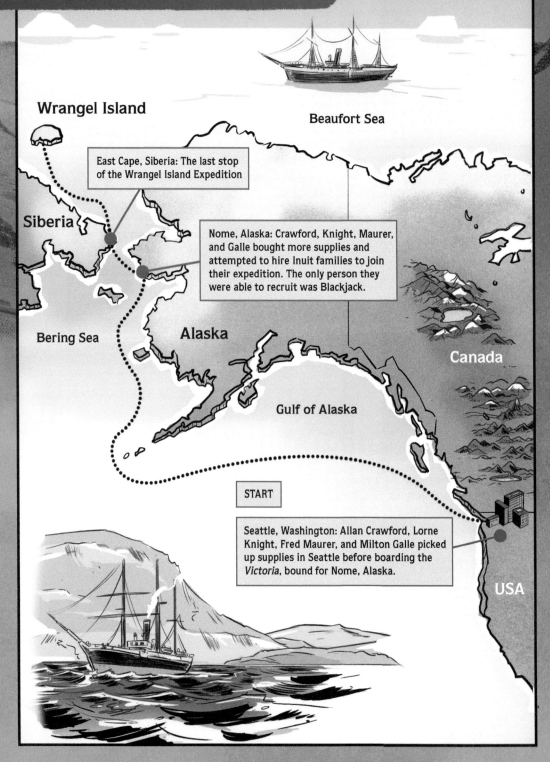

Wrangel Island

Beaufort Sea

East Cape, Siberia: The last stop of the Wrangel Island Expedition

Siberia

Nome, Alaska: Crawford, Knight, Maurer, and Galle bought more supplies and attempted to hire Inuit families to join their expedition. The only person they were able to recruit was Blackjack.

Bering Sea

Alaska

Gulf of Alaska

Canada

START

Seattle, Washington: Allan Crawford, Lorne Knight, Fred Maurer, and Milton Galle picked up supplies in Seattle before boarding the *Victoria*, bound for Nome, Alaska.

USA

MORE ABOUT THE EXPEDITION

Vilhjalmur Stefansson was heavily criticized for sending such an unprepared crew on the Wrangel Island expedition.

No sign of Maurer, Galle, or Crawford was ever found. They were presumed dead. In 1924, Canada and Britain announced that they did not hold a claim on Wrangel Island.

Stefansson published *The Adventure of Wrangel Island* in 1925. He claimed the trip was Maurer and Knight's idea. He described the men as clumsy and unskilled. The parents of the four men were upset at how their sons were represented in the book. Crawford's parents published a statement blaming Stefansson for their son's death.

Blackjack rarely spoke about her experience. She gave one interview in Los Angeles in 1924 and would not give another for nearly 50 years. She only did so in 1973 at the request of her son Billy.

Harold Noice later claimed in newspaper articles that Blackjack had mistreated and starved Knight instead of caring for the sick man. But Knight's parents, who had befriended Blackjack, never believed these lies.

GLOSSARY

colony (KAH-luh-nee)—an area that has been settled by people from another country; a colony is ruled by another country

expedition (ek-spuh-DI-shuhn)—a group of people on a journey with a goal, such as starting a settlement on a deserted Arctic island

Inuit (IN-yoo-ut)—the native people of Alaska and other northern and Arctic regions; the singular form of Inuit is Inuk

missionary (MISH-uh-ner-ee)—a person who works on behalf of a religious group to spread the group's faith

native (NAY-tuhv)—people who originally lived in a certain place

orphanage (OR-fuh-nij)—a place that provides a home for children whose parents have died or can no longer care for them

scurvy (SKUR-vee)—a deadly disease caused by lack of vitamin C; scurvy produces swollen limbs, bleeding gums, and weakness

tuberculosis (tu-BUR-kyoo-low-sis)—a disease caused by bacteria that causes fever, weight loss, and coughing; left untreated, tuberculosis can lead to death

READ MORE

Huang, Nellie. *Explorers: Amazing Tales of the World's Greatest Adventurers.* New York: DK Publishing, 2019.

Loh-Hagan, Virginia. *Ada Blackjack: Castaway.* Ann Arbor, MI: Cherry Lake, 2018.

Simons, Lisa M. Bolt. *The Vanished Northwest Passage Arctic Expedition.* North Mankato, MN: Capstone, 2022.

INTERNET SITES

Ada Blackjack, the Forgotten Sole Survivor of an Odd Arctic Expedition
atlasobscura.com/articles/ada-blackjack-arctic-survivor

The Death of Ada Blackjack
nunatsiaq.com/stories/article/taissumani_may_29_1983_the_death_of_ada_blackjack/

The Inuit Woman Who Survived the Arctic Alone
outsideonline.com/2274756/inuit-woman-who-survived-arctic-alone

INDEX

AUTHOR BIO

Dr. Katrina Phillips is a citizen of the Red Cliff Band of Lake Superior Ojibwe. She earned her BA and PhD in History from the University of Minnesota, and she teaches Native American history and the history of the American West at Macalester College.

ILLUSTRATOR BIO

Dave Shephard is a comic book artist and illustrator of children's books. He's tried doing other things, but none of them quite cut the mustard.